DAMASK

BELVEDERE

DAMASK

From the Classic Fabric Collection

ARRANGED AND EDITED BY WOLFGANG H. HAGENEY

PUBLICATIONS INTERNATIONAL, ROME/ITALY

DAMASK - *a luxurious and verdant silken fabric beloved of the Church and feted by the rich and wealthy people who would use it very often as a buttress for their status.*

DAMASK

Published by
Belvedere Publications, Int.
Rome, Italy.

© COPYRIGHT 1995 by
Belvedere Publications
International, Inc.
First published 1995 (1st edition)

Printed in Italy by
Il Centro Stampa, Rome.
Color Separations by
Centro Cromografico, Rome.
Films & Lithography by
Belvedere Laboratories.
Typesetting by
Centro TypeSet Belvedere,
Rome, Italy.
Bound by: Allestimento
Grafico Biotto, Pomezia

Layout & Styling by
Belvedere Studio Productions.
Art Direction: HWH & BVR
Artwork/Graphic Design:
Studio Belvedere
Graphic Designer:
Katia Dimonte
Print & Studio Production:
Rosa B. Lengsfeld
Editor & Publisher:
Wolfgang H. Hageney

DAMASK

is part of the
Belvedere Publications
series, which include:
Belvedere Design-Books,
Designer's Notebooks,
Cad-Books, Archi-Books,
Culture-Design-Books,
Grafix, Ref.-Books, ExPressArt.
The Creative Image Bank,
Active Graphic Design,
Art Studio, IdeaBooks,
Classic Clip Art Collection,
Impulse, Mix Magazine,
which are all ® registered
trademarks.

BELVEDERE PUBLICATIONS
INTERNATIONAL, INC.
I - 00135 ROME / ITALY
P.O.BOX - C.P. 12.301
TEL. (+39-6) 35.50.55.31 / 42
FAX (+39-6) 35.50.55.55

ISBN 88-7070-101-8

DAMASCUS,

geographically, was one of the crossroads of the ancient Arab empires. Along the thousands of miles of track and road which stretched to Timbuktoo, Samarkand, Sian, Kashgar, Turfan and distant Cathay all kinds of cargoes, from slaves to precious metals made their weary, profitable, hazardous ways.

Numbered among the treasures of this old world were fabrics: a new form of currency, particular to their peculiar extractions. In these the peoples of the Silk Road, as it became later known, found and treasured silks, originally brought across the world as feather-weight armour by the Mongols. Now, Mongol dealers proffered skeins of yarn, something revolutionary and innovatory, a military secret, and as with all old military technologies, merchants saw new uses for ageing techniques. With the interface between the old uses and the new concepts, in a strange land with different parameters and unknown agendas, the silk traders changed the horizon: combining ancient ideas and modern methods a dynamic product was extracted from the expanding cultural hothouse of the Arabic reverie, something tradeable and rare, something desirable and precious, yet mass productable and constant: it became known as Damascus, much as De Nimes would be spoken of much later. From all the dust and toil and flux of the old world *Damask* had been born.

To the occidental consciousness the word Damascus, itself almost a dusky transition, represented an industry of quality textiles, which, arising in the city which gave it it's name in Syria in the early middle ages, serviced the then Byzantine market situated along the eastern shores of the burgeoning Mediterranean. Demand created a situation where the original production in Damascus became limited, geographical boundaries such as deserts created communication and profitability problems: so production swiftly moved into nearby accessible areas, almost certainly by sea. *Damask* in terms of industrial production had arrived at Lucca, Italy by the 13th century and in France by the 16th Century. A luxurious and verdant silken fabric beloved of the Church and feted by the rich and wealthy people who would use it very often as a buttress for their status.

By this time methods of production had changed, perhaps affected by associated industrial developments in Europe, and undoubtedly by the relative coarseness of many medieval European materials. The fabric itself had altered, affected by the varying conditions which obtained overseas, so that the production of cotton Damask became common, though the highest quality in this general area of fabric was and still often is produced from linen which gives a sheen which is similar to that of silk, but with a tougher, more hard wearing, quality.

In the 19th century *Damask* was being produced using the revolutionary Jacquard method, this time with wool, and now mainly for furnishings and warm clothing. The prelude to true mass production using these early computer-like techniques. At their inception the vast majority of damasks had been simple monotonal fabrics, using sculpting and cross-webbing to create highly dramatic and rather theatrical effects. As thinking improved however, other colors were added to the original grounds: Jacquarding being the typical method. Gradually the development of other forms of textile manipulation at machine stage allowed the multifarious use of color in the creation of the new, modern Damasks, something previously only possible by hand stitching and painstakingly slow work. The Damascus of the old world had transformed itself into the *Damask* of the new.

*The motifs of the present volume
derive from several original design collections,
which offer a rich choice of typical
decorative Damask motifs.*

*The comprehensive selection contains
striking masterpieces of Floral Motifs,
beautiful Ornaments, colorful Decorations,
a variety of classical Border Designs
as well as historical Panels and old styled
Geometric & Heraldic Patterns.*

*This edition was re-arranged & re-created by
the Belvedere Studio in Rome, Italy.*

9

10

12

14

18

19

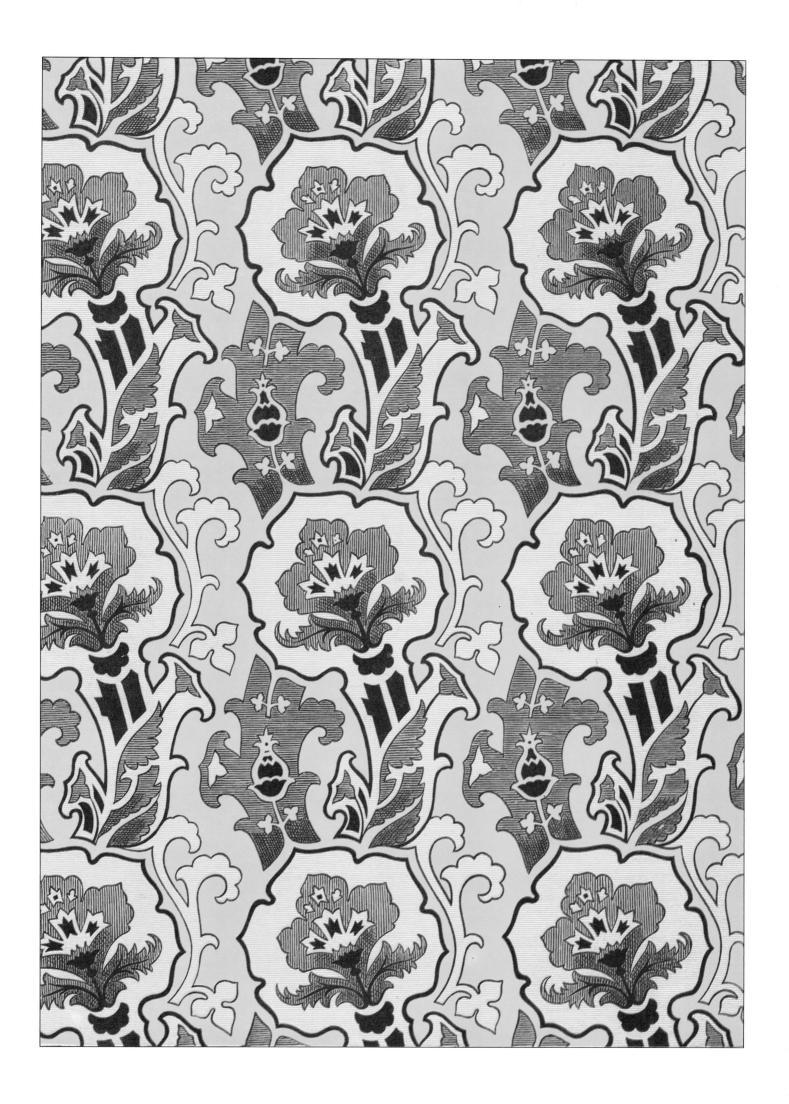

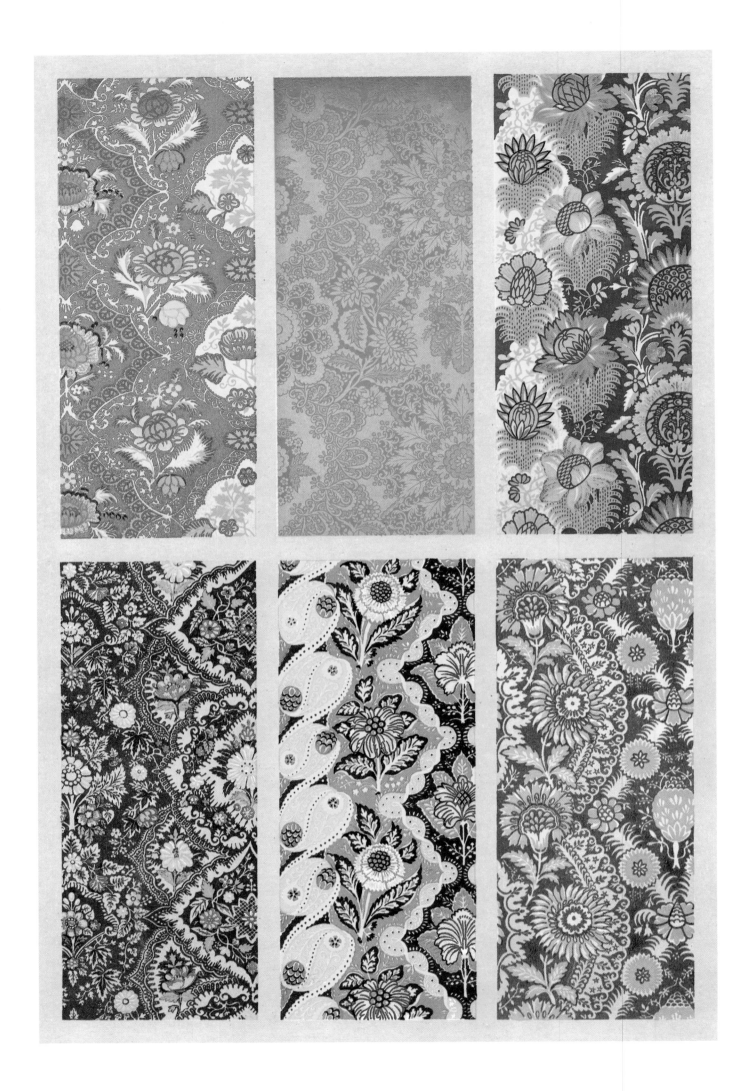

34

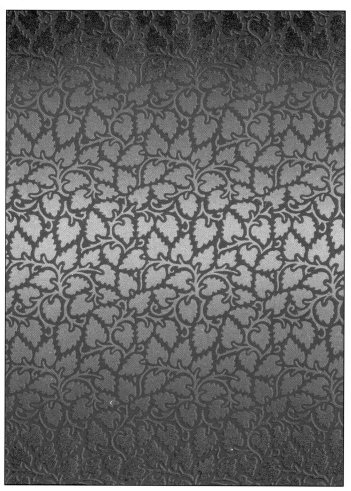 

44

46

56

64

66

67

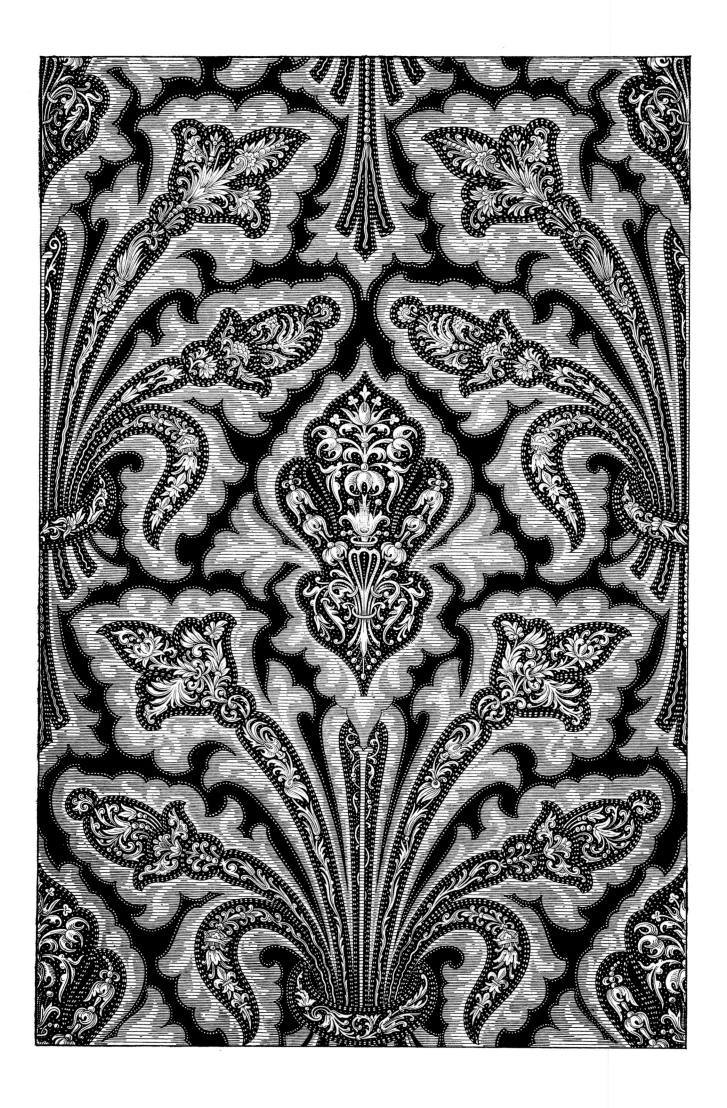

74

78

BELVEDERE PUBLICATIONS
presents

ETHNIC

DESIGNS & MOTIFS
IN A WIDE RANGE OF BOOKS
AND DIFFERENT THEMES.
GENERAL FOLK & ETHNIC IDEAS
FROM ALL OVER THE WORLD,
TEXTILES & DESIGNS
FROM AFRICA,
MOTIFS FROM THE TREASURE OF
THE NATIVE AMERICANS.

•

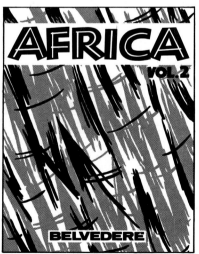

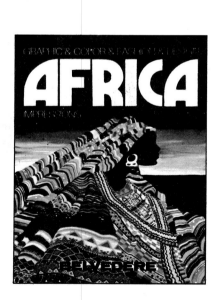

The legendary best-seller of the Edition BELVEDERE, "BLACK AFRICA", is available not only in a complete hardcover edition, but also in two single and handy paperbacks, which form the same contents as the hardcover edition. An impressive book of Fashion, Textiles, Color, Graphic and Design.

PROFESSIONAL DESIGN BOOKS
FOR THE FIELD OF
TEXTILE AND FASHION,
CREATIVE GRAPHIC DESIGN,
CULTURAL HANDICRAFTS
OR FOR ANY KIND OF
VISUAL COMMUNICATION.
GO AND ASK FOR THE
GENERAL CATALOG
OF ALL THE BELVEDERE
PUBLICATIONS.

PRACTICAL PAPERBACK EDITIONS
FOR THE PROFESSIONAL USE.
RETURNING TO THE
AGE OF PRIMITIVE CULTURES.
ETHNIC FOR FASHION,
FUN & FUNCTION.
DESIGNS IN LARGE
FORMATS. READY TO
USE. CREATIVE SOURCES.
A WORLD OF FANTASY.
B/W & COLOR.

CREATIVE • DESIGN • IDEAS

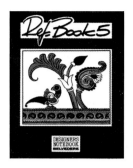

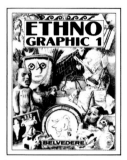

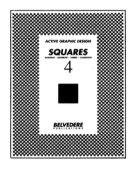
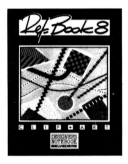

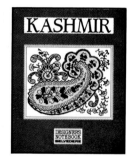

FASHION•TEXTILE•BOOKS

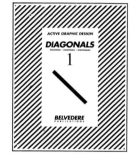

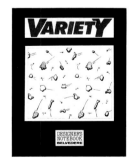

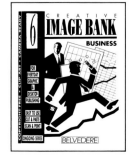

PRACTICAL · GRAPHIC · ART

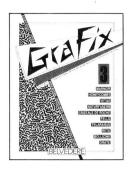
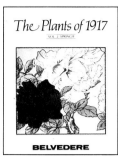

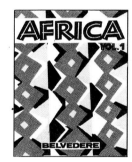

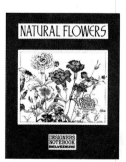
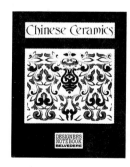

COLOR • SOURCE • BOOKS

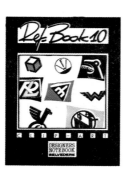

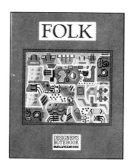

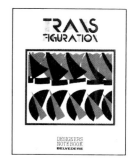

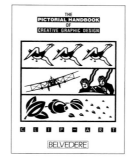

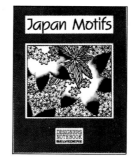

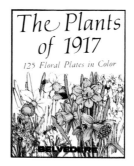

CLIP-ART

COMPUTER • SCANNER • CAMERA

Super tools for professionals & creative artists.
Ready to use images, patterns, designs and textures.
High resolution reproduction & print quality.

A wide range of graphic motifs, not only simply the best in its field, but also cost efficient and better than any of its kind.

COPYRIGHT-FREE

If you want to be a member of the BELVEDERE DESIGN CLUB International...

GOOD DESIGN BOOKS ARE HARD TO FIND. IT TAKES YOU TIME AND MONEY TO GET THE RIGHT IMAGES AND IDEAS, REFERENCES OR TOOLS YOU NEED FOR YOUR CREATIVE / PRACTICAL ART WORK. BUT NOW YOU CAN HAVE IT ALL MORE EASILY. CHOOSE SIMPLY THE BEST IN ITS FIELD: THE BELVEDERE-DESIGN-BOOKS, "MADE IN ITALY".
GO, AND ASK RIGHT NOW FOR THE "DESIGN CLUB" AND YOU WILL GET A VERY SPECIAL OFFER (FREE OF CHARGE) IMMEDIATELY. IT WILL SURPRISE YOU. WRITE, CALL OR FAX, OR SEND SIMPLY THE DESIGN-CLUB CARD TO ROME, ITALY FOR FURTHER INFORMATION OR FOR A FULL CATALOG. WE WILL DO ALL THE REST FOR YOU.

É DIFFICILE TROVARE BUONI LIBRI DI DESIGN. CI VUOLE TEMPO E DENARO PER AVERE LE IMMAGINI E LE IDEE GIUSTE. MA ADESSO É TUTTO PIÚ FACILE. SCEGLIETE SOLAMENTE IL MEGLIO: I LIBRI • DESIGN DELLA EDIZIONE BELVEDERE, "MADE IN ITALY". CHIEDETE DEL DESIGN-CLUB INTERNATIONAL E AVRETE SUBITO GRATIS DELLE OFFERTE ECCEZIONALI CHE VI SORPRENDERANNO. MANDATE SEMPLICEMENTE LA CARTOLINA ACCANTO CON LA POSTA O VIA FAX PER RICEVERE ULTERIORI INFORMAZIONI O UN CATALOGO.

IN'EST PAS FACILE DE TROUVER DE BONS OUVRAGES DE DESSIN. VOUS AVEZ SANS DOUTE SOUVENT PERDU BEAU-COUP DE TEMPS ET D'ARGENT DANS LA RECHERCHE D'IMAGES & D'IDÉES NOUVELLES. AUJOURD'HUI CELA VOUS SERA PLUS FACILE. CHOISISSEZ TOUJOURS LE MEILLEUR: LES BELVEDERE DESIGN-BOOKS, "MADE IN ITALY". ÉCRIVEZ AU DESIGN-CLUB ET VOUS RECEVREZ GRATIS, ET PAR RETOUR DU CORRIER UNE OFFRE SPÉCIALE QUI VOUS SURPRENDERA AGRÉABLEMENT.

GUTE DESIGN BÜCHER SIND SCHWIERIG ZU FINDEN. ES ER-FORDERT OFT VIEL ZEIT UND GELD, UM AN DIE RICHTIGEN IDEEN UND VORLAGEN ZU GELANGEN. DOCH JETZT IST DIES ALLES VIEL LEICHTER. WÄHLEN SIE EINFACH DAS BESTE: DIE BELVEDERE DESIGN-BÜCHER, "MADE IN ITALY". ERKUNDIGEN SIE SICH NACH DEM DESIGN-CLUB INTERNATIONAL UND SIE WERDEN UNVERZÜGLICH UND KOSTENLOS EIN SPEZIAL-ANGEBOT ERHALTEN, DAS SIE ÜBERRASCHEN WIRD. ALLES ANDERE BESORGT FÜR SIE BELVEDERE.

ES REALMENTE DIFÍCIL ENCONTRAR BUENOS LIBROS DE DESIGN. SE NECESITAN TIEMPO Y DINERO PARA OBTENER LAS IMÁGENES & IDEAS APROPIADAS PARA VUESTRO TRABAJO. AHORA TODO ES MÁS FACIL. PUEDE CONSEGUIRSE LO MEJOR CON LOS BELVEDERE-DESIGN-BOOKS, "MADE IN ITALY". ES SUFICIENTE SOLICITARLOS AL DESIGN-CLUB INTERNACIONAL; INMEDIATAMENTE, Y GRATIS, RECIBIRÉIS MERAVILLOSAS OFERTAS.